TROMBONE
101 POPULAR SONGS

Available for
FLUTE, CLARINET, ALTO SAX, TENOR SAX, TRUMPET,
HORN, TROMBONE, VIOLIN, VIOLA, CELLO

ISBN 978-1-4950-9029-5

For all works contained herein:
Unauthorized copying, arranging, adapting, recording, Internet posting, public performance,
or other distribution of the printed music in this publication is an infringement of copyright.
Infringers are liable under the law.

HAL•LEONARD®

Visit Hal Leonard Online at **www.halleonard.com**

Explore the entire family of Hal Leonard products and resources

World headquarters, contact:
Hal Leonard
7777 West Bluemound Road
Milwaukee, WI 53213
Email: info@halleonard.com

In Europe, contact:
Hal Leonard Europe Limited
1 Red Place
London, W1K 6PL
Email: info@halleonardeurope.com

In Australia, contact:
Hal Leonard Australia Pty. Ltd.
4 Lentara Court
Cheltenham, Victoria, 3192 Australia
Email: info@halleonard.com.au

CONTENTS

ABC

TROMBONE

Words and Music by ALPHONSO MIZELL,
FREDERICK PERREN, DEKE RICHARDS
and BERRY GORDY

Copyright © 1970 Jobete Music Co., Inc.
Copyright Renewed
All Rights Administered by Sony/ATV Music Publishing LLC, 424 Church Street, Suite 1200, Nashville, TN 37219
International Copyright Secured   All Rights Reserved

AFTERNOON DELIGHT

TROMBONE

Words and Music by
BILL DANOFF

Moderately slow, in 2

Copyright © 1976 BMG Ruby Songs and Reservoir Media Management, Inc.
Copyright Renewed
All Rights for BMG Ruby Songs Administered by BMG Rights Management (US) LLC
All Rights for Reservoir Media Management, Inc. Administered by Alfred Music
All Rights Reserved   Used by Permission

AIN'T NO SUNSHINE

TROMBONE

Words and Music by
BILL WITHERS

Copyright © 1971 INTERIOR MUSIC CORP.
Copyright Renewed
All Rights Controlled and Administered by SONGS OF UNIVERSAL, INC.
All Rights Reserved   Used by Permission

ALL YOU NEED IS LOVE

TROMBONE

Words and Music by JOHN LENNON
and PAUL McCARTNEY

Copyright © 1967 Sony/ATV Music Publishing LLC
Copyright Renewed
All Rights Administered by Sony/ATV Music Publishing LLC, 424 Church Street, Suite 1200, Nashville, TN 37219
International Copyright Secured   All Rights Reserved

AIN'T TOO PROUD TO BEG

TROMBONE

Words and Music by EDWARD HOLLAND JR.
and NORMAN WHITFIELD

Copyright © 1966 Jobete Music Co., Inc.
Copyright Renewed
All Rights Administered by Sony/ATV Music Publishing LLC on behalf of Stone Agate Music (A Division of Jobete Music Co., Inc.),
424 Church Street, Suite 1200, Nashville, TN 37219
International Copyright Secured   All Rights Reserved

ALL NIGHT LONG
(All Night)

TROMBONE

Words and Music by
LIONEL RICHIE

Copyright © 1983 by Brockman Music and Brenda Richie Publishing
All Rights Reserved   Used by Permission

ANOTHER BRICK IN THE WALL

TROMBONE

Words and Music by
ROGER WATERS

Moderately

Copyright © 1979 Roger Waters Music Overseas Ltd.
All Rights Administered by BMG Rights Management (US) LLC
All Rights Reserved   Used by Permission

AT SEVENTEEN

TROMBONE

Words and Music by
JANIS IAN

© 1975 (Renewed 2003) MINE MUSIC LTD.
All Rights for the U.S.A. and Canada Controlled and Administered by EMI APRIL MUSIC INC.
All Rights Reserved International Copyright Secured Used by Permission

BAD, BAD LEROY BROWN

TROMBONE

Words and Music by
JIM CROCE

Copyright © 1972 (Renewed 2000) Time In A Bottle Publishing and Croce Publishing
All Rights Administered by BMG Rights Management (US) LLC
All Rights Reserved   Used By Permission

BIG GIRLS DON'T CRY

TROMBONE

Words and Music by BOB CREWE
and BOB GAUDIO

Moderately

© 1962, 1963 (Renewed) CLARIDGE MUSIC COMPANY, A Division of MPL Music Publishing, Inc.
All Rights Reserved

BILLIE JEAN

TROMBONE

Words and Music by
MICHAEL JACKSON

Moderately bright

Copyright © 1982 Mijac Music
All Rights Administered by Sony/ATV Music Publishing LLC, 424 Church Street, Suite 1200, Nashville, TN 37219
International Copyright Secured   All Rights Reserved

BRIDGE OVER TROUBLED WATER

TROMBONE

Words and Music by
PAUL SIMON

Moderately

Copyright © 1969 Paul Simon (BMI)
Copyright Renewed
International Copyright Secured   All Rights Reserved
Used by Permission

CALIFORNIA DREAMIN'

TROMBONE

Words and Music by JOHN PHILLIPS
and MICHELLE PHILLIPS

Copyright © 1965 UNIVERSAL MUSIC CORP.
Copyright Renewed
All Rights Reserved   Used by Permission

CARIBBEAN QUEEN
(No More Love on the Run)

TROMBONE

Words and Music by KEITH VINCENT ALEXANDER
and BILLY OCEAN

Copyright © 1984 by Universal Music - Z Songs, Keith Diamond Music and Aqua Music Ltd.
All Rights for Keith Diamond Music Administered by Universal Music - Z Songs
All Rights for Aqua Music Ltd. Administered in the United States and Canada by Universal Music - Z Tunes LLC
International Copyright Secured   All Rights Reserved

CENTERFOLD

TROMBONE

Words and Music by
SETH JUSTMAN

Bright Rock

© 1981 CENTER CITY MUSIC and PAL-PARK MUSIC
All Rights for CENTER CITY MUSIC Administered by BMG RIGHTS MANAGEMENT (US) LLC
All Rights for PAL-PARK MUSIC Administered by ALMO MUSIC CORP.
All Rights Reserved   Used by Permission

COPACABANA
(At the Copa)

TROMBONE

Music by BARRY MANILOW
Lyric by BRUCE SUSSMAN and JACK FELDMAN

Moderately, with a Latin feel

Copyright © 1978 by Universal Music - Careers, Appoggiatura Music and Camp Songs
All Rights Administered by Universal Music - Careers
International Copyright Secured   All Rights Reserved

CRACKLIN' ROSIE

TROMBONE

Words and Music by
NEIL DIAMOND

Copyright © 1970 PROPHET MUSIC, INC.
Copyright Renewed
All Rights Administered by UNIVERSAL TUNES
All Rights Reserved   Used by Permission

DO YOU BELIEVE IN MAGIC

TROMBONE

Words and Music by
JOHN SEBASTIAN

Copyright © 1965 by Alley Music Corp. and Trio Music Company
Copyright Renewed
All Rights for Trio Music Company Administered by BMG Rights Management (US) LLC
International Copyright Secured   All Rights Reserved
Used by Permission

DOWNTOWN

TROMBONE

Words and Music by
TONY HATCH

Copyright © 1964, 1965 WELBECK MUSIC LTD.
Copyright Renewed
All Rights in the United States and Canada Controlled and Administered by SONGS OF UNIVERSAL, INC.
All Rights Reserved   Used by Permission

DOWN UNDER

TROMBONE

Words and Music by COLIN HAY
and RON STRYKERT

© 1982 EMI SONGS AUSTRALIA PTY. LIMITED
All Rights in the United States Controlled and Administered by EMI BLACKWOOD MUSIC INC.
All Rights Reserved   International Copyright Secured   Used by Permission

DUST IN THE WIND

TROMBONE

Words and Music by
KERRY LIVGREN

Copyright © 1977, 1978 EMI Blackwood Music Inc. and Don Kirshner Music
Copyright Renewed
All Rights Administered by Sony/ATV Music Publishing LLC, 424 Church Street, Suite 1200, Nashville, TN 37219
International Copyright Secured   All Rights Reserved

THE FIRST TIME EVER I SAW YOUR FACE

TROMBONE

Words and Music by
EWAN MacCOLL

Copyright © 1962, 1966 by Stormking Music Inc.
Copyright Renewed and Assigned to Ewan MacColl Ltd.
All Rights for the USA Administered by David Platz Music Inc.
All Rights Reserved   Used by Permission

EASY

TROMBONE

Words and Music by
LIONEL RICHIE

Copyright © 1977 Jobete Music Co., Inc. and Libren Music
Copyright Renewed
All Rights Administered by Sony/ATV Music Publishing LLC, 424 Church Street, Suite 1200, Nashville, TN 37219
International Copyright Secured   All Rights Reserved

FREE BIRD

TROMBONE

Words and Music by ALLEN COLLINS
and RONNIE VAN ZANT

Copyright © 1973, 1975 SONGS OF UNIVERSAL, INC.
Copyrights Renewed
All Rights Reserved   Used by Permission

GENTLE ON MY MIND

TROMBONE

Words and Music by
JOHN HARTFORD

Copyright © 1967, 1968 Sony/ATV Music Publishing LLC
Copyright Renewed
All Rights Administered by Sony/ATV Music Publishing LLC, 424 Church Street, Suite 1200, Nashville, TN 37219
International Copyright Secured   All Rights Reserved

GIRLS JUST WANT TO HAVE FUN

TROMBONE

Words and Music by
ROBERT HAZARD

Copyright © 1979 Sony/ATV Music Publishing LLC
All Rights Administered by Sony/ATV Music Publishing LLC, 424 Church Street, Suite 1200, Nashville, TN 37219
International Copyright Secured   All Rights Reserved

GOD ONLY KNOWS

TROMBONE

Words and Music by BRIAN WILSON
and TONY ASHER

Copyright © 1966 IRVING MUSIC, INC.
Copyright Renewed
All Rights Reserved   Used by Permission

GROOVIN'

TROMBONE

Words and Music by FELIX CAVALIERE
and EDWARD BRIGATI, JR.

© 1967 (Renewed 1995) EMI JEMAXAL MUSIC INC., JONATHAN THREE MUSIC and DELICIOUS APPLE MUSIC CORP.
All Rights Reserved   International Copyright Secured   Used by Permission

HAPPY TOGETHER

TROMBONE

Words and Music by GARRY BONNER
and ALAN GORDON

Copyright © 1966, 1967 by Alley Music Corp. and Trio Music Company
Copyright Renewed
All Rights for Trio Music Company Administered by BMG Rights Management (US) LLC
International Copyright Secured   All Rights Reserved
Used by Permission

HEY JUDE

TROMBONE

Words and Music by JOHN LENNON
and PAUL McCARTNEY

Slowly

Copyright © 1968 Sony/ATV Music Publishing LLC
Copyright Renewed
All Rights Administered by Sony/ATV Music Publishing LLC, 424 Church Street, Suite 1200, Nashville, TN 37219
International Copyright Secured   All Rights Reserved

I GET AROUND

TROMBONE

Words and Music by BRIAN WILSON
and MIKE LOVE

Copyright © 1964 IRVING MUSIC, INC.
Copyright Renewed
All Rights Reserved   Used by Permission

I HEARD IT THROUGH THE GRAPEVINE

TROMBONE

Words and Music by NORMAN J. WHITFIELD
and BARRETT STRONG

Copyright Renewed
All Rights Administered by Sony/ATV Music Publishing LLC on behalf of Stone Agate Music (A Division of Jobete Music Co., Inc.),
424 Church Street, Suite 1200, Nashville, TN 37219
International Copyright Secured   All Rights Reserved

I SAW HER STANDING THERE

TROMBONE

Words and Music by JOHN LENNON
and PAUL McCARTNEY

Copyright © 1963 by NORTHERN SONGS LTD., London, England
Copyright Renewed
All Rights for the U.S.A., its territories and possessions and Canada assigned to and controlled by GIL MUSIC CORP., 1650 Broadway, New York, NY 10019
International Copyright Secured   All Rights Reserved

I STILL HAVEN'T FOUND WHAT I'M LOOKING FOR

TROMBONE

Words and Music by
U2

Copyright © 1987 UNIVERSAL MUSIC PUBLISHING INTERNATIONAL B.V.
All Rights in the United States and Canada Controlled and Administered by UNIVERSAL - POLYGRAM INTERNATIONAL PUBLISHING, INC.
All Rights Reserved   Used by Permission

I'M A BELIEVER

TROMBONE

Words and Music by
NEIL DIAMOND

Moderately fast

Copyright © 1966 TALLYRAND MUSIC, INC. and EMI FORAY MUSIC
Copyright Renewed
All Rights for TALLYRAND MUSIC, INC. Administered by UNIVERSAL TUNES
All Rights for EMI FORAY MUSIC Administered by SONY/ATV MUSIC PUBLISHING LLC, 424 Church Street, Suite 1200, Nashville, TN 37219
All Rights Reserved   Used by Permission

I WILL SURVIVE

TROMBONE

Words and Music by DINO FEKARIS
and FREDERICK J. PERREN

Moderately

Copyright © 1978 UNIVERSAL - POLYGRAM INTERNATIONAL PUBLISHING, INC. and PERREN-VIBES MUSIC, INC.
All Rights Controlled and Administered by UNIVERSAL - POLYGRAM INTERNATIONAL PUBLISHING, INC.
All Rights Reserved   Used by Permission

IF

TROMBONE

Words and Music by
DAVID GATES

Moderately, with feeling

Copyright © 1971 Sony/ATV Music Publishing LLC
Copyright Renewed
All Rights Administered by Sony/ATV Music Publishing LLC, 424 Church Street, Suite 1200, Nashville, TN 37219
International Copyright Secured   All Rights Reserved

IMAGINE

TROMBONE

Words and Music by
JOHN LENNON

© 1971 (Renewed) LENONO MUSIC
All Rights Administered by DOWNTOWN DMP SONGS/DOWNTOWN MUSIC PUBLISHING LLC
All Rights Reserved   Used by Permission

JESSIE'S GIRL

TROMBONE

Words and Music by
RICK SPRINGFIELD

Moderately fast

Copyright © 1981 UNIVERSAL - SONGS OF POLYGRAM INTERNATIONAL, INC.
All Rights Reserved   Used by Permission

JUST ONCE

TROMBONE

Words by CYNTHIA WEIL
Music by BARRY MANN

Copyright © 1981 Sony/ATV Music Publishing LLC and Mann & Weil Songs, Inc.
All Rights Administered by Sony/ATV Music Publishing LLC, 424 Church Street, Suite 1200, Nashville, TN 37219
International Copyright Secured   All Rights Reserved

KARMA CHAMELEON

TROMBONE

Words and Music by GEORGE O'DOWD,
JONATHAN MOSS, MICHAEL CRAIG,
ROY HAY and PHIL PICKETT

Moderately fast

Copyright © 1983 BMG VM Music Ltd. and Pendulum Music Ltd.
All Rights for BMG VM Music Ltd. Administered by BMG Rights Management (US) LLC
All Rights for Pendulum Music Ltd. for the World Controlled by Warner Bros. Music Ltd.
All Rights for Warner Bros. Music Ltd. for the Western Hemisphere, except Brazil, Administered by Warner-Tamerlane Publishing Corp.
All Rights Reserved   Used by Permission

KILLING ME SOFTLY WITH HIS SONG

Words by NORMAN GIMBEL
Music by CHARLES FOX

TROMBONE

Moderately

© 1972 (Renewed) RODALI MUSIC and WORDS WEST LLC (P.O. Box 15187, Beverly Hills, CA 90209 USA)
All Rights for RODALI MUSIC Administered by WARNER-TAMERLANE PUBLISHING CORP.
All Rights Reserved   Used by Permission

LADY

TROMBONE

Words and Music by
LIONEL RICHIE

Copyright © 1980 by Brockman Music and Brenda Richie Publishing
All Rights Reserved   Used by Permission

LAY DOWN SALLY

TROMBONE

Words and Music by ERIC CLAPTON,
MARCY LEVY and GEORGE TERRY

Copyright © 1977 by Eric Patrick Clapton and Throat Music Ltd.
Copyright Renewed
All Rights for Throat Music Ltd. Administered by Unichappell Music Inc.
International Copyright Secured   All Rights Reserved

LEADER OF THE PACK

TROMBONE

Words and Music by GEORGE MORTON,
JEFF BARRY and ELLIE GREENWICH

© 1964 (Renewed 1992) SCREEN GEMS-EMI MUSIC INC. and TENDER TUNES MUSIC CO.
All Rights Controlled and Administered by SCREEN GEMS-EMI MUSIC INC.
All Rights Reserved   International Copyright Secured   Used by Permission

LEAN ON ME

TROMBONE

Words and Music by
BILL WITHERS

Copyright © 1972 INTERIOR MUSIC CORP.
Copyright Renewed
All Rights Controlled and Administered by SONGS OF UNIVERSAL, INC.
All Rights Reserved   Used by Permission

LEAVING ON A JET PLANE

TROMBONE

Words and Music by
JOHN DENVER

Copyright © 1967; Renewed 1995 BMG Ruby Songs and Reservoir Media Music
All Rights for BMG Ruby Songs Administered by BMG Rights Management (US) LLC
All Rights for Reservoir Media Music Administered by Reservoir Media Management, Inc. (Publishing) and Alfred Music (Print)
All Rights Reserved   Used by Permission

LET'S HANG ON

TROMBONE

Words and Music by BOB CREWE,
DENNY RANDELL and SANDY LINZER

Copyright © 1965 Screen Gems-EMI Music Inc., Saturday Music and Seasons Four Music
Copyright Renewed
All Rights on behalf of Screen Gems-EMI Music Inc. and Saturday Music Administered by
Sony/ATV Music Publishing LLC, 424 Church Street, Suite 1200, Nashville, TN 37219
International Copyright Secured   All Rights Reserved

LET'S HEAR IT FOR THE BOY

from the Paramount Motion Picture FOOTLOOSE

TROMBONE

Words by DEAN PITCHFORD
Music by TOM SNOW

Copyright © 1984 Sony/ATV Melody LLC
All Rights by Sony/ATV Music Publishing LLC, 424 Church Street, Suite 1200, Nashville, TN 37219
International Copyright Secured   All Rights Reserved

LIKE A VIRGIN

TROMBONE

Words and Music by BILLY STEINBERG
and TOM KELLY

Copyright © 1984 Sony/ATV Music Publishing LLC
All Rights Administered by Sony/ATV Music Publishing LLC, 424 Church Street, Suite 1200, Nashville, TN 37219
International Copyright Secured   All Rights Reserved

THE LION SLEEPS TONIGHT

TROMBONE

New Lyrics and Revised Music by GEORGE DAVID WEISS,
HUGO PERETTI and LUIGI CREATORE

© 1961 FOLKWAYS MUSIC PUBLISHERS, INC.
Copyright Renewed by GEORGE DAVID WEISS, LUIGI CREATORE and JUNE PERETTI
Copyright Assigned to ABILENE MUSIC LLC
All Rights Administered Worldwide by IMAGEM MUSIC LLC
All Rights Reserved   Used by Permission

LIVIN' ON A PRAYER

TROMBONE

Words and Music by JON BON JOVI,
DESMOND CHILD and RICHIE SAMBORA

Copyright © 1986 Bon Jovi Publishing, Universal - PolyGram International Publishing, Inc., Sony/ATV Music Publishing LLC and Aggressive Music
All Rights for Bon Jovi Publishing Administered Worldwide by Kobalt Songs Music Publishing
All Rights for Sony/ATV Music Publishing LLC and Aggressive Music Administered by Sony/ATV Music Publishing LLC, 424 Church Street, Suite 1200, Nashville, TN 37219
All Rights Reserved   Used by Permission

LOVE WILL KEEP US TOGETHER

TROMBONE

Words and Music by NEIL SEDAKA
and HOWARD GREENFIELD

Copyright © 1973 R2M Music, Songs Of SJL-RSL Music Co., Universal Music - Careers and EMI Sosaha Music Inc.
Copyright Renewed
All Rights for R2M Music Administered by BMG Rights Management (US) LLC
All Rights for EMI Sosaha Music Inc. Administered by Sony/ATV Music Publishing LLC, 424 Church Street, Suite 1200, Nashville, TN 37219
All Rights Reserved   Used by Permission

MANDY

TROMBONE

Words and Music by SCOTT ENGLISH
and RICHARD KERR

Copyright © 1971 Screen Gems-EMI Music Ltd. and Graphle Music Ltd.
Copyright Renewed
All Rights on behalf of Screen Gems-EMI Music Ltd. Administered by Sony/ATV Music Publishing LLC, 424 Church Street, Suite 1200, Nashville, TN 37219
All Rights on behalf of Graphle Music Ltd. Administered in the U.S. and Canada by Morris Music, Inc.
International Copyright Secured   All Rights Reserved

MANEATER

TROMBONE

**Words and Music by SARA ALLEN,
DARYL HALL and JOHN OATES**

Copyright © 1982 Geomantic Music, Hot Cha Music Co. and Unichappell Music, Inc.
All Rights for Geomantic Music and Hot Cha Music Co. Administered by BMG Rights Management (US) LLC
All Rights Reserved   Used by Permission

MR. TAMBOURINE MAN

TROMBONE

Words and Music by
BOB DYLAN

Copyright © 1964, 1965 Warner Bros. Inc.
Copyright Renewed 1992, 1996 Special Rider Music
International Copyright Secured   All Rights Reserved
Reprinted by Permission of Music Sales Corporation

MONDAY, MONDAY

TROMBONE

Words and Music by
JOHN PHILLIPS

Copyright © 1966 UNIVERSAL MUSIC CORP.
Copyright Renewed
All Rights Reserved   Used by Permission

MONY, MONY

TROMBONE

Words and Music by BOBBY BLOOM,
TOMMY JAMES, RITCHIE CORDELL
and BO GENTRY

© 1968 (Renewed 1996) EMI LONGITUDE MUSIC
All Rights Reserved   International Copyright Secured   Used by Permission

MY CHERIE AMOUR

TROMBONE

Words and Music by STEVIE WONDER,
SYLVIA MOY and HENRY COSBY

Copyright © 1968 Jobete Music Co., Inc. and Black Bull Music
Copyright Renewed
All Rights Administered by Sony/ATV Music Publishing LLC, 424 Church Street, Suite 1200, Nashville, TN 37219
International Copyright Secured   All Rights Reserved

MY GIRL

TROMBONE

Words and Music by SMOKEY ROBINSON
and RONALD WHITE

Moderately

Copyright © 1964 Jobete Music Co., Inc.
Copyright Renewed
All Rights Administered by Sony/ATV Music Publishing LLC, 424 Church Street, Suite 1200, Nashville, TN 37219
International Copyright Secured   All Rights Reserved

NIGHTS IN WHITE SATIN

TROMBONE

Words and Music by
JUSTIN HAYWARD

Slowly, in 2

© Copyright 1967 (Renewed), 1968 (Renewed) and 1970 (Renewed) Tyler Music Ltd., London, England
TRO - Essex Music, Inc., New York, controls all publication rights for the U.S.A. and Canada
International Copyright Secured
All Rights Reserved Including Public Performance For Profit
Used by Permission

NIGHTSHIFT

TROMBONE

Words and Music by WALTER ORANGE,
FRANNE GOLDE and DENNIS LAMBERT

Copyright © 1985 Reservoir Media Music, VMG World Wide and Universal Music - Careers
All Rights for Reservoir Media Music Administered by Reservoir Media Management, Inc.
All Rights for VMG World Wide Administered by BMG Rights Management (US) LLC
All Rights Reserved   Used by Permission

ONE MORE NIGHT

TROMBONE

Words and Music by
PHIL COLLINS

Moderately slow, in 2

To Coda ⊕   1.   2.   **D.C. al Coda (take repeat)**   **CODA** ⊕

Copyright © 1984 Phil Collins Ltd. and Imagem CV
All Rights Reserved   Used by Permission

PHYSICAL

TROMBONE

Words and Music by STEPHEN A. KIPNER
and TERRY SHADDICK

Copyright © 1981 EMI April Music Inc. and Terry Shaddick Music
All Rights on behalf of EMI April Music Inc. Administered by Sony/ATV Music Publishing LLC, 424 Church Street, Suite 1200, Nashville, TN 37219
International Copyright Secured   All Rights Reserved

PIANO MAN

TROMBONE

Words and Music by
BILLY JOEL

Moderately slow, in 1

Copyright © 1973 JOELSONGS
Copyright Renewed
All Rights Administered by ALMO MUSIC CORP.
All Rights Reserved   Used by Permission

POUR SOME SUGAR ON ME

TROMBONE

Words and Music by JOE ELLIOTT,
PHIL COLLEN, RICHARD SAVAGE,
RICHARD ALLEN, STEVE CLARK
and R.J. LANGE

Copyright © 1987 Bludgeon Riffola Ltd. and Out Of Pocket Productions Ltd.
All Rights for Bludgeon Riffola Ltd. Administered by BMG Rights Management (US) LLC
All Rights for Out Of Pocket Productions Ltd. Administered by Universal - PolyGram International Publishing, Inc.
All Rights Reserved   Used by Permission

REELING IN THE YEARS

TROMBONE

Words and Music by WALTER BECKER
and DONALD FAGEN

Copyright © 1972, 1973 UNIVERSAL MUSIC CORP. and RED GIANT, INC.
Copyrights Renewed
All Rights Controlled and Administered by UNIVERSAL MUSIC CORP.
All Rights Reserved   Used by Permission

RIGHT HERE WAITING

TROMBONE

Words and Music by
RICHARD MARX

Copyright © 1989 BMG Monarch
All Rights Administered by BMG Rights Management (US) LLC
All Rights Reserved   Used by Permission

ROCKET MAN
(I Think It's Gonna Be a Long Long Time)

TROMBONE

Words and Music by ELTON JOHN
and BERNIE TAUPIN

Slowly, in 2

Copyright © 1972 UNIVERSAL/DICK JAMES MUSIC LTD.
Copyright Renewed
All Rights in the United States and Canada Controlled and Administered by UNIVERSAL - SONGS OF POLYGRAM INTERNATIONAL, INC.
All Rights Reserved   Used by Permission

SAVING ALL MY LOVE FOR YOU

TROMBONE

Words by GERRY GOFFIN
Music by MICHAEL MASSER

Slowly, in 2

© 1978, 1985 SCREEN GEMS-EMI MUSIC INC., LAUREN-WESLEY MUSIC INC. and UNIVERSAL MUSIC CORP.
All Rights for LAUREN-WESLEY MUSIC INC. Controlled and Administered by SCREEN GEMS-EMI MUSIC INC.
All Rights Reserved   International Copyright Secured   Used by Permission

SHE DRIVES ME CRAZY

TROMBONE

Words and Music by DAVID STEELE
and ROLAND GIFT

Copyright © 1988 BMG VM Music Ltd.
All Rights Administered by BMG Rights Management (US) LLC
All Rights Reserved   Used by Permission

SHINY HAPPY PEOPLE

TROMBONE

Words and Music by WILLIAM BERRY,
PETER BUCK, MICHAEL MILLS
and MICHAEL STIPE

Copyright © 1991 NIGHT GARDEN
All Rights Administered by SONGS OF UNIVERSAL, INC.
All Rights Reserved   Used by Permission

SILLY LOVE SONGS

TROMBONE

Words and Music by PAUL McCARTNEY
and LINDA McCARTNEY

© 1976 (Renewed) MPL COMMUNICATIONS LTD.
Administered by MPL COMMUNICATIONS, INC.
All Rights Reserved

D.C. al Coda

CODA

SISTER CHRISTIAN

TROMBONE

Words and Music by
KELLY KEAGY

Copyright © 1983 by Figs. D Music and Rough Play Music
All Rights Administered by Figs. D Music c/o The Bicycle Music Company
All Rights Reserved   Used by Permission

(Sittin' On)
THE DOCK OF THE BAY

TROMBONE

Words and Music by STEVE CROPPER
and OTIS REDDING

Copyright © 1968, 1975 IRVING MUSIC, INC.
Copyright Renewed
All Rights for the world outside the U.S. Controlled and Administered by WB MUSIC CORP. and IRVING MUSIC, INC.
All Rights Reserved   Used by Permission

SMOKE ON THE WATER

TROMBONE

Words and Music by RITCHIE BLACKMORE,
IAN GILLAN, ROGER GLOVER,
JON LORD and IAN PAICE

Copyright © 1972 B. Feldman & Co. Ltd.
Copyright Renewed
All Rights Administered by Sony/ATV Music Publishing LLC, 424 Church Street, Suite 1200, Nashville, TN 37219
International Copyright Secured   All Rights Reserved

SOMEBODY TO LOVE

TROMBONE

Words and Music by
FREDDIE MERCURY

Moderately, in 2

Copyright © 1976 Queen Music Ltd.
Copyright Renewed
All Rights Administered by Sony/ATV Music Publishing LLC, 424 Church Street, Suite 1200, Nashville, TN 37219
International Copyright Secured   All Rights Reserved

SON-OF-A-PREACHER MAN

TROMBONE

Words and Music by JOHN HURLEY
and RONNIE WILKINS

Moderately, in 2

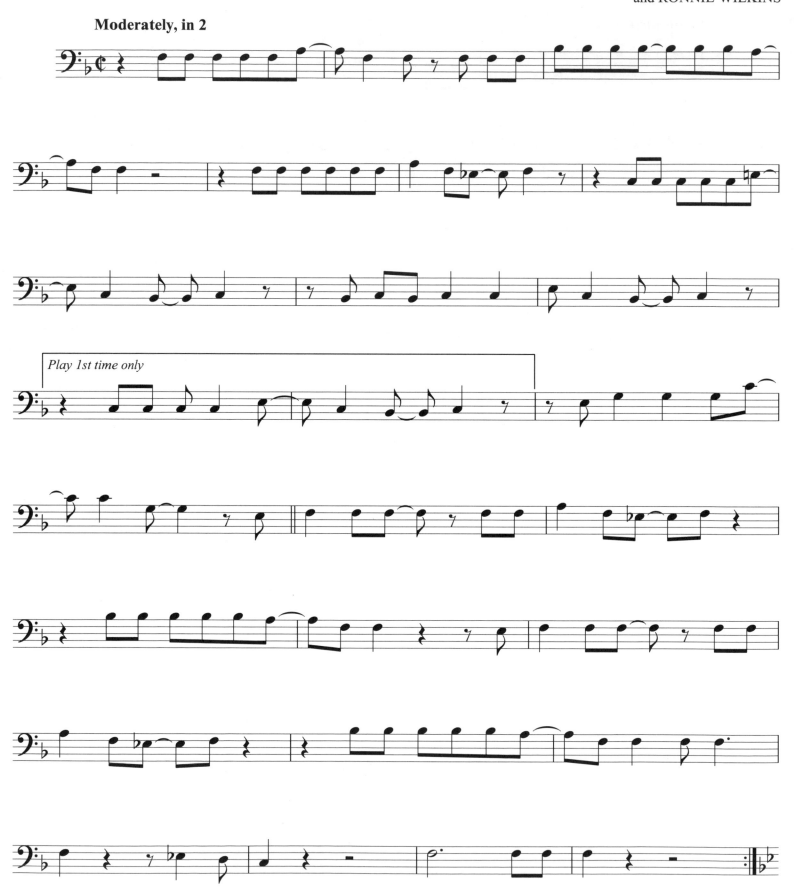

Play 1st time only

Copyright © 1968 Sony/ATV Music Publishing LLC
Copyright Renewed
All Rights Administered by Sony/ATV Music Publishing LLC, 424 Church Street, Suite 1200, Nashville, TN 37219
International Copyright Secured   All Rights Reserved

THE SOUND OF SILENCE

TROMBONE

Words and Music by
PAUL SIMON

Copyright © 1964 Paul Simon (BMI)
International Copyright Secured   All Rights Reserved
Used by Permission

STAND BY ME

TROMBONE

Words and Music by JERRY LEIBER,
MIKE STOLLER and BEN E. KING

Moderately, with a beat

Copyright © 1961 Sony/ATV Music Publishing LLC
Copyright Renewed
All Rights Administered by Sony/ATV Music Publishing LLC, 424 Church Street, Suite 1200, Nashville, TN 37219
International Copyright Secured   All Rights Reserved

SWEET DREAMS
(Are Made of This)

TROMBONE

Words and Music by ANNIE LENNOX
and DAVID STEWART

Moderately

Copyright © 1983 by Universal Music Publishing MGB Ltd.
All Rights in the U.S. and Canada Administered by Universal Music - MGB Songs
International Copyright Secured   All Rights Reserved

SWEET HOME ALABAMA

TROMBONE

Words and Music by RONNIE VAN ZANT,
ED KING and GARY ROSSINGTON

Copyright © 1974 SONGS OF UNIVERSAL, INC., EMI LONGITUDE MUSIC, UNIVERSAL MUSIC CORP. and FULL KEEL MUSIC
Copyright Renewed
All Rights Controlled and Administered by SONGS OF UNIVERSAL, INC. and UNIVERSAL MUSIC CORP.
All Rights Reserved   Used by Permission

TAKE ME HOME, COUNTRY ROADS

TROMBONE

Words and Music by JOHN DENVER,
BILL DANOFF and TAFFY NIVERT

Copyright © 1971; Renewed 1999 BMG Ruby Songs, My Pop's Songs, Dino Park Publishing, Jesse Belle Denver and Reservoir Media Music in the U.S.
All Rights for BMG Ruby Songs Administered by BMG Rights Management (US) LLC
All Rights for My Pop's Songs and Dino Park Publishing Administered by Kobalt Songs Music Publishing
All Rights for Jesse Belle Denver Administered by WB Music Corp.
All Rights for Reservoir Media Music Administered by Reservoir Media Management, Inc. (Publishing) and Alfred Music (Print)
All Rights Reserved   Used by Permission

THESE DREAMS

TROMBONE

Words and Music by MARTIN GEORGE PAGE
and BERNIE TAUPIN

Moderately slow, in 2

Copyright © 1985 LITTLE MOLE MUSIC and IMAGEM LONDON LTD.
All Rights for LITTLE MOLE MUSIC in the U.S. and Canada Controlled and Administered by UNIVERSAL - POLYGRAM INTERNATIONAL PUBLISHING, INC.
All Rights for IMAGEM LONDON LTD. in the U.S. and Canada Controlled and Administered by UNIVERSAL MUSIC - Z TUNES LLC
All Rights Reserved   Used by Permission

THROUGH THE YEARS

TROMBONE

Words and Music by STEVE DORFF
and MARTY PANZER

Copyright © 1980 by Universal Music - Careers and SwaneeBRAVO! Music
International Copyright Secured   All Rights Reserved

TICKET TO RIDE

TROMBONE

Words and Music by JOHN LENNON
and PAUL McCARTNEY

Copyright © 1965 Sony/ATV Music Publishing LLC
Copyright Renewed
All Rights Administered by Sony/ATV Music Publishing LLC, 424 Church Street, Suite 1200, Nashville, TN 37219
International Copyright Secured   All Rights Reserved

TIME AFTER TIME

TROMBONE

Words and Music by CYNDI LAUPER
and ROB HYMAN

Copyright © 1983 Rellla Music Co. and Dub Notes
All Rights for Rellla Music Co. Administered by Sony/ATV Music Publishing LLC, 424 Church Street, Suite 1200, Nashville, TN 37219
All Rights for Dub Notes Administered by WB Music Corp.
International Copyright Secured   All Rights Reserved

TIME IN A BOTTLE

Words and Music by
JIM CROCE

TROMBONE

Copyright © 1971 (Renewed 1999) Time In A Bottle Publishing and Croce Publishing
All Rights Administered by BMG Rights Management (US) LLC
All Rights Reserved   Used by Permission

TRAVELIN' MAN

TROMBONE

Words and Music by
JERRY FULLER

Moderately

Copyright © 1960 Sony/ATV Music Publishing LLC
Copyright Renewed
All Rights Administered by Sony/ATV Music Publishing LLC, 424 Church Street, Suite 1200, Nashville, TN 37219
International Copyright Secured   All Rights Reserved

25 OR 6 TO 4

TROMBONE

Words and Music by
ROBERT LAMM

Copyright © 1970 Lamminations Music and Spirit Catalog Holdings, S.a.r.l.
Copyright Renewed
All Rights for Lamminations Music Administered by BMG Rights Management (US) LLC
All Rights for Spirit Catalog Holdings, S.a.r.l. Controlled and Administered by Spirit Two Music, Inc.
International Copyright Secured All Rights Reserved

UP, UP AND AWAY

TROMBONE

Words and Music by
JIMMY WEBB

Copyright © 1967 R2M Music
Copyright Renewed
All Rights Administered by BMG Rights Management (US) LLC
All Rights Reserved   Used by Permission

WE'RE NOT GONNA TAKE IT

TROMBONE

Words and Music by
DANIEL DEE SNIDER

Copyright © 1984 by Universal Music - Z Melodies and Snidest Music
All Rights in the United States Administered by Universal Music - Z Melodies
International Copyright Secured   All Rights Reserved

WHAT'S LOVE GOT TO DO WITH IT

TROMBONE

Words and Music by GRAHAM LYLE
and TERRY BRITTEN

Copyright © 1984 Goodsingle Limited and WB Music Corp.
All Rights for Goodsingle Limited Administered in the U.S. and Canada by Songs Of Kobalt Music Publishing
All Rights Reserved   Used by Permission

A WHITER SHADE OF PALE

TROMBONE

Words and Music by KEITH REID,
GARY BROOKER and MATTHEW FISHER

© Copyright 1967 (Renewed) Onward Music Ltd., London, England
TRO - Essex Music, Inc., New York, controls all publication rights for the U.S.A. and Canada
International Copyright Secured
All Rights Reserved Including Public Performance For Profit
Used by Permission

WICHITA LINEMAN

TROMBONE

Words and Music by
JIMMY WEBB

Copyright © 1968 UNIVERSAL - POLYGRAM INTERNATIONAL PUBLISHING, INC.
Copyright Renewed
All Rights Reserved   Used by Permission

WITH OR WITHOUT YOU

TROMBONE

Words and Music by
U2

Moderately

Copyright © 1987 UNIVERSAL MUSIC PUBLISHING INTERNATIONAL B.V.
All Rights in the United States and Canada Controlled and Administered by UNIVERSAL - POLYGRAM INTERNATIONAL PUBLISHING, INC.
All Rights Reserved   Used by Permission

YESTERDAY

TROMBONE

Words and Music by JOHN LENNON
and PAUL McCARTNEY

Copyright © 1965 Sony/ATV Music Publishing LLC
Copyright Renewed
All Rights Administered by Sony/ATV Music Publishing LLC, 424 Church Street, Suite 1200, Nashville, TN 37219
International Copyright Secured   All Rights Reserved

YOU ARE SO BEAUTIFUL

TROMBONE

Words and Music by BILLY PRESTON
and BRUCE FISHER

Copyright © 1973 IRVING MUSIC, INC. and ALMO MUSIC CORP.
Copyright Renewed
All Rights Reserved   Used by Permission

YOU CAN'T HURRY LOVE

TROMBONE

Words and Music by EDWARD HOLLAND JR.,
LAMONT DOZIER and BRIAN HOLLAND

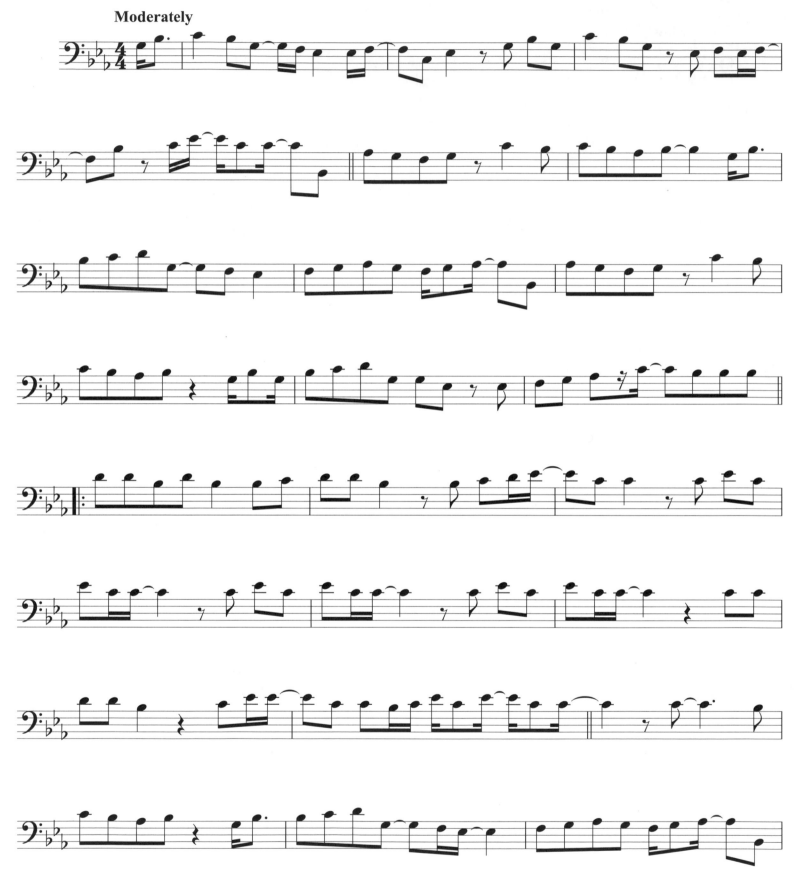

Copyright © 1965 Jobete Music Co., Inc.
Copyright Renewed
All Rights Administered by Sony/ATV Music Publishing LLC on behalf of Stone Agate Music
(A Division of Jobete Music Co., Inc.), 424 Church Street, Suite 1200, Nashville, TN 37219
International Copyright Secured   All Rights Reserved

YOU REALLY GOT ME

TROMBONE

Words and Music by
RAY DAVIES

Moderately

Copyright © 1964 Jayboy Music Corp.
Copyright Renewed
All Rights Administered by Sony/ATV Music Publishing LLC, 424 Church Street, Suite 1200, Nashville, TN 37219
International Copyright Secured   All Rights Reserved

YOU'RE SO VAIN

TROMBONE

Words and Music by
CARLY SIMON

Copyright © 1972 C'est Music
Copyright Renewed
All Rights Administered by BMG Rights Management (US) LLC
All Rights Reserved   Used by Permission

101 SONGS

BIG COLLECTIONS OF FAVORITE SONGS
ARRANGED FOR SOLO INSTRUMENTALISTS.

101 BROADWAY SONGS

00154199	Flute	$15.99
00154200	Clarinet	$15.99
00154201	Alto Sax	$15.99
00154202	Tenor Sax	$16.99
00154203	Trumpet	$15.99
00154204	Horn	$15.99
00154205	Trombone	$15.99
00154206	Violin	$15.99

00154207 Viola.................................$15.99
00154208 Cello.................................$15.99

101 DISNEY SONGS

00244104	Flute	$17.99
00244106	Clarinet	$17.99
00244107	Alto Sax	$17.99
00244108	Tenor Sax	$17.99
00244109	Trumpet	$17.99
00244112	Horn	$17.99
00244120	Trombone	$17.99
00244121	Violin	$17.99

00244125 Viola.................................$17.99
00244126 Cello.................................$17.99

101 MOVIE HITS

00158087	Flute	$15.99
00158088	Clarinet	$15.99
00158089	Alto Sax	$15.99
00158090	Tenor Sax	$15.99
00158091	Trumpet	$15.99
00158092	Horn	$15.99
00158093	Trombone	$15.99
00158094	Violin	$15.99

00158095 Viola.................................$15.99
00158096 Cello.................................$15.99

101 CHRISTMAS SONGS

00278637	Flute	$15.99
00278638	Clarinet	$15.99
00278639	Alto Sax	$15.99
00278640	Tenor Sax	$15.99
00278641	Trumpet	$15.99
00278642	Horn	$14.99
00278643	Trombone	$15.99
00278644	Violin	$15.99

00278645 Viola.................................$15.99
00278646 Cello.................................$15.99

101 HIT SONGS

00194561	Flute	$17.99
00197182	Clarinet	$17.99
00197183	Alto Sax	$17.99
00197184	Tenor Sax	$17.99
00197185	Trumpet	$17.99
00197186	Horn	$17.99
00197187	Trombone	$17.99
00197188	Violin	$17.99

00197189 Viola.................................$17.99
00197190 Cello.................................$17.99

101 POPULAR SONGS

00224722	Flute	$17.99
00224723	Clarinet	$17.99
00224724	Alto Sax	$17.99
00224725	Tenor Sax	$17.99
00224726	Trumpet	$17.99
00224727	Horn	$17.99
00224728	Trombone	$17.99
00224729	Violin	$17.99

00224730 Viola.................................$17.99
00224731 Cello.................................$17.99

101 CLASSICAL THEMES

00155315	Flute	$15.99
00155317	Clarinet	$15.99
00155318	Alto Sax	$15.99
00155319	Tenor Sax	$15.99
00155320	Trumpet	$15.99
00155321	Horn	$15.99
00155322	Trombone	$15.99
00155323	Violin	$15.99

00155324 Viola.................................$15.99
00155325 Cello.................................$15.99

101 JAZZ SONGS

00146363	Flute	$15.99
00146364	Clarinet	$15.99
00146366	Alto Sax	$15.99
00146367	Tenor Sax	$15.99
00146368	Trumpet	$15.99
00146369	Horn	$14.99
00146370	Trombone	$15.99
00146371	Violin	$15.99

00146372 Viola.................................$15.99
00146373 Cello.................................$15.99

101 MOST BEAUTIFUL SONGS

00291023	Flute	$16.99
00291041	Clarinet	$16.99
00291042	Alto Sax	$17.99
00291043	Tenor Sax	$17.99
00291044	Trumpet	$16.99
00291045	Horn	$16.99
00291046	Trombone	$16.99
00291047	Violin	$16.99

00291048 Viola.................................$16.99
00291049 Cello.................................$17.99

See complete song lists and sample pages at www.halleonard.com

HAL•LEONARD®
www.halleonard.com

Prices, contents and availability subject to change without notice.

Hal•Leonard INSTRUMENTAL PLAY-ALONG

Your favorite songs are arranged just for solo instrumentalists with this outstanding series. Each book includes great full-accompaniment play-along audio so you can sound just like a pro!

Check out **halleonard.com** for songlists and more titles!

12 Pop Hits
12 songs
00261790	Flute	00261795	Horn
00261791	Clarinet	00261796	Trombone
00261792	Alto Sax	00261797	Violin
00261793	Tenor Sax	00261798	Viola
00261794	Trumpet	00261799	Cello

The Very Best of Bach
15 selections
00225371	Flute	00225376	Horn
00225372	Clarinet	00225377	Trombone
00225373	Alto Sax	00225378	Violin
00225374	Tenor Sax	00225379	Viola
00225375	Trumpet	00225380	Cello

The Beatles
15 songs
00225330	Flute	00225335	Horn
00225331	Clarinet	00225336	Trombone
00225332	Alto Sax	00225337	Violin
00225333	Tenor Sax	00225338	Viola
00225334	Trumpet	00225339	Cello

Chart Hits
12 songs
00146207	Flute	00146212	Horn
00146208	Clarinet	00146213	Trombone
00146209	Alto Sax	00146214	Violin
00146210	Tenor Sax	00146211	Trumpet
00146216	Cello		

Christmas Songs
12 songs
00146855	Flute	00146863	Horn
00146858	Clarinet	00146864	Trombone
00146859	Alto Sax	00146866	Violin
00146860	Tenor Sax	00146867	Viola
00146862	Trumpet	00146868	Cello

Contemporary Broadway
15 songs
00298704	Flute	00298709	Horn
00298705	Clarinet	00298710	Trombone
00298706	Alto Sax	00298711	Violin
00298707	Tenor Sax	00298712	Viola
00298708	Trumpet	00298713	Cello

Disney Movie Hits
12 songs
00841420	Flute	00841424	Horn
00841687	Oboe	00841425	Trombone
00841421	Clarinet	00841426	Violin
00841422	Alto Sax	00841427	Viola
00841686	Tenor Sax	00841428	Cello
00841423	Trumpet		

Prices, contents, and availability subject to change without notice.

Disney characters and artwork ™ & © 2021 Disney

Disney Solos
12 songs
00841404	Flute	00841506	Oboe
00841406	Alto Sax	00841409	Trumpet
00841407	Horn	00841410	Violin
00841411	Viola	00841412	Cello
00841405	Clarinet/Tenor Sax		
00841408	Trombone/Baritone		
00841553	Mallet Percussion		

Dixieland Favorites
15 songs
00268756	Flute	0068759	Trumpet
00268757	Clarinet	00268760	Trombone
00268758	Alto Sax		

Billie Eilish
9 songs
00345648	Flute	00345653	Horn
00345649	Clarinet	00345654	Trombone
00345650	Alto Sax	00345655	Violin
00345651	Tenor Sax	00345656	Viola
00345652	Trumpet	00345657	Cello

Favorite Movie Themes
13 songs
00841166	Flute	00841168	Trumpet
00841167	Clarinet	00841170	Trombone
00841169	Alto Sax	00841296	Violin

Gospel Hymns
15 songs
00194648	Flute	00194654	Trombone
00194649	Clarinet	00194655	Violin
00194650	Alto Sax	00194656	Viola
00194651	Tenor Sax	00194657	Cello
00194652	Trumpet		

Great Classical Themes
15 songs
00292727	Flute	00292733	Horn
00292728	Clarinet	00292735	Trombone
00292729	Alto Sax	00292736	Violin
00292730	Tenor Sax	00292737	Viola
00292732	Trumpet	00292738	Cello

The Greatest Showman
8 songs
00277389	Flute	00277394	Horn
00277390	Clarinet	00277395	Trombone
00277391	Alto Sax	00277396	Violin
00277392	Tenor Sax	00277397	Viola
00277393	Trumpet	00277398	Cello

Irish Favorites
31 songs
00842489	Flute	00842495	Trombone
00842490	Clarinet	00842496	Violin
00842491	Alto Sax	00842497	Viola
00842493	Trumpet	00842498	Cello
00842494	Horn		

Michael Jackson
11 songs
00119495	Flute	00119499	Trumpet
00119496	Clarinet	00119501	Trombone
00119497	Alto Sax	00119503	Violin
00119498	Tenor Sax	00119502	Accomp.

Jazz & Blues
14 songs
00841438	Flute	00841441	Trumpet
00841439	Clarinet	00841443	Trombone
00841440	Alto Sax	00841444	Violin
00841442	Tenor Sax		

Jazz Classics
12 songs
00151812	Flute	00151816	Trumpet
00151813	Clarinet	00151818	Trombone
00151814	Alto Sax	00151819	Violin
00151815	Tenor Sax	00151821	Cello

Les Misérables
13 songs
00842292	Flute	00842297	Horn
00842293	Clarinet	00842298	Trombone
00842294	Alto Sax	00842299	Violin
00842295	Tenor Sax	00842300	Viola
00842296	Trumpet	00842301	Cello

Metallica
12 songs
02501327	Flute	02502454	Horn
02501339	Clarinet	02501329	Trombone
02501332	Alto Sax	02501334	Violin
02501333	Tenor Sax	02501335	Viola
02501330	Trumpet	02501338	Cello

Motown Classics
15 songs
00842572	Flute	00842576	Trumpet
00842573	Clarinet	00842578	Trombone
00842574	Alto Sax	00842579	Violin
00842575	Tenor Sax		

Pirates of the Caribbean
16 songs
00842183	Flute	00842188	Horn
00842184	Clarinet	00842189	Trombone
00842185	Alto Sax	00842190	Violin
00842186	Tenor Sax	00842191	Viola
00842187	Trumpet	00842192	Cello

Queen
17 songs
00285402	Flute	00285407	Horn
00285403	Clarinet	00285408	Trombone
00285404	Alto Sax	00285409	Violin
00285405	Tenor Sax	00285410	Viola
00285406	Trumpet	00285411	Cello

Simple Songs
14 songs
00249081	Flute	00249087	Horn
00249093	Oboe	00249089	Trombone
00249082	Clarinet	00249090	Violin
00249083	Alto Sax	00249091	Viola
00249084	Tenor Sax	00249092	Cello
00249086	Trumpet	00249094	Mallets

Superhero Themes
14 songs
00363195	Flute	00363200	Horn
00363196	Clarinet	00363201	Trombone
00363197	Alto Sax	00363202	Violin
00363198	Tenor Sax	00363203	Viola
00363199	Trumpet	00363204	Cello

Star Wars
16 songs
00350900	Flute	00350907	Horn
00350913	Oboe	00350908	Trombone
00350903	Clarinet	00350909	Violin
00350904	Alto Sax	00350910	Viola
00350905	Tenor Sax	00350911	Cello
00350906	Trumpet	00350914	Mallet

Taylor Swift
15 songs
00842532	Flute	00842537	Horn
00842533	Clarinet	00842538	Trombone
00842534	Alto Sax	00842539	Violin
00842535	Tenor Sax	00842540	Viola
00842536	Trumpet	00842541	Cello

Video Game Music
13 songs
00283877	Flute	00283883	Horn
00283878	Clarinet	00283884	Trombone
00283879	Alto Sax	00283885	Violin
00283880	Tenor Sax	00283886	Viola
00283882	Trumpet	00283887	Cello

Wicked
13 songs
00842236	Flute	00842241	Horn
00842237	Clarinet	00842242	Trombone
00842238	Alto Sax	00842243	Violin
00842239	Tenor Sax	00842244	Viola
00842240	Trumpet	00842245	Cello

101 TIPS FROM HAL LEONARD

STUFF ALL THE PROS KNOW AND USE

Ready to take your skills to the next level? These books present valuable how-to insight that musicians of all styles and levels can benefit from. The text, photos, music, diagrams and accompanying audio provide a terrific, easy-to-use resource for a variety of topics.

101 HAMMOND B-3 TIPS
by Brian Charette
Topics include: funky scales and modes; unconventional harmonies; creative chord voicings; cool drawbar settings; ear-grabbing special effects; professional gigging advice; practicing effectively; making good use of the pedals; and much more!
00128918 Book/Online Audio $14.99

101 HARMONICA TIPS
by Steve Cohen
Topics include: techniques, position playing, soloing, accompaniment, the blues, equipment, performance, maintenance, and much more!
00821040 Book/Online Audio $17.99

101 CELLO TIPS—2ND EDITION
by Angela Schmidt
Topics include: bowing techniques, non-classical playing, electric cellos, accessories, gig tips, practicing, recording and much more!
00149094 Book/Online Audio $14.99

101 FLUTE TIPS
by Elaine Schmidt
Topics include: selecting the right flute for you, finding the right teacher, warm-up exercises, practicing effectively, taking good care of your flute, gigging advice, staying and playing healthy, and much more.
00119883 Book/CD Pack...................................$14.99

101 SAXOPHONE TIPS
by Eric Morones
Topics include: techniques; maintenance; equipment; practicing; recording; performance; and much more!
00311082 Book/CD Pack...................................$19.99

101 TRUMPET TIPS
by Scott Barnard
Topics include: techniques, articulation, tone production, soloing, exercises, special effects, equipment, performance, maintenance and much more.
00312082 Book/CD Pack...................................$14.99

101 UPRIGHT BASS TIPS
by Andy McKee
Topics include: right- and left-hand technique, improvising and soloing, practicing, proper care of the instrument, ear training, performance, and much more.
00102009 Book/Online Audio $14.99

101 BASS TIPS
by Gary Willis
Topics include: techniques, improvising and soloing, equipment, practicing, ear training, performance, theory, and much more.
00695542 Book/Online Audio $19.99

101 DRUM TIPS—2ND EDITION
Topics include: grooves, practicing, warming up, tuning, gear, performance, and much more!
00151936 Book/Online Audio $14.99

101 FIVE-STRING BANJO TIPS
by Fred Sokolow
Topics include: techniques, ear training, performance, and much more!
00696647 Book/CD Pack...................................$14.99

101 GUITAR TIPS
by Adam St. James
Topics include: scales, music theory, truss rod adjustments, proper recording studio set-ups, and much more. The book also features snippets of advice from some of the most celebrated guitarists and producers in the music business.
00695737 Book/Online Audio $17.99

101 MANDOLIN TIPS
by Fred Sokolow
Topics include: playing tips, practicing tips, accessories, mandolin history and lore, practical music theory, and much more!
00119493 Book/Online Audio $14.99

101 RECORDING TIPS
by Adam St. James
This book contains recording tips, suggestions, and advice learned firsthand from legendary producers, engineers, and artists. These tricks of the trade will improve anyone's home or pro studio recordings.
00311035 Book/CD Pack...................................$14.95

101 UKULELE TIPS
by Fred Sokolow with Ronny Schiff
Topics include: techniques, improvising and soloing, equipment, practicing, ear training, performance, uke history and lore, and much more!
00696596 Book/Online Audio $15.99

101 VIOLIN TIPS
by Angela Schmidt
Topics include: bowing techniques, non-classical playing, electric violins, accessories, gig tips, practicing, recording, and much more!
00842672 Book/CD Pack...................................$14.99

Prices, contents and availability subject to change without notice.

HAL•LEONARD®
www.halleonard.com

THE ULTIMATE COLLECTION OF
FAKE BOOKS

The Real Book – Sixth Edition

Hal Leonard proudly presents the first legitimate and legal editions of these books ever produced. These bestselling titles are mandatory for anyone who plays jazz! Over 400 songs, including: All By Myself • Dream a Little Dream of Me • God Bless the Child • Like Someone in Love • When I Fall in Love • and more.

00240221 Volume 1, C Instruments.....................$45.00
00240224 Volume 1, B♭ Instruments....................$45.00
00240225 Volume 1, E♭ Instruments....................$45.00
00240226 Volume 1, BC Instruments....................$45.00

Go to halleonard.com
to view all *Real Books* available

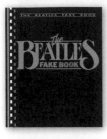

The Beatles Fake Book

200 of the Beatles' hits: All You Need Is Love • Blackbird • Can't Buy Me Love • Day Tripper • Eleanor Rigby • The Fool on the Hill • Hey Jude • In My Life • Let It Be • Michelle • Norwegian Wood (This Bird Has Flown) • Penny Lane • Revolution • She Loves You • Twist and Shout • With a Little Help from My Friends • Yesterday • and many more!
00240069 C Instruments...........$39.99

The Best Fake Book Ever

More than 1,000 songs from all styles of music: All My Loving • At the Hop • Cabaret • Dust in the Wind • Fever • Hello, Dolly • Hey Jude • King of the Road • Longer • Misty • Route 66 • Sentimental Journey • Somebody • Song Sung Blue • Spinning Wheel • Unchained Melody • We Will Rock You • What a Wonderful World • Wooly Bully • Y.M.C.A. • and more.

00290239 C Instruments...............$49.99
00240084 E♭ Instruments..............$49.95

The Celtic Fake Book

Over 400 songs from Ireland, Scotland and Wales: Auld Lang Syne • Barbara Allen • Danny Boy • Finnegan's Wake • The Galway Piper • Irish Rover • Loch Lomond • Molly Malone • My Bonnie Lies Over the Ocean • My Wild Irish Rose • That's an Irish Lullaby • and more. Includes Gaelic lyrics where applicable and a pronunciation guide.
00240153 C Instruments...........$25.00

Classic Rock Fake Book

Over 250 of the best rock songs of all time: American Woman • Beast of Burden • Carry On Wayward Son • Dream On • Free Ride • Hurts So Good • I Shot the Sheriff • Layla • My Generation • Nights in White Satin • Owner of a Lonely Heart • Rhiannon • Roxanne • Summer of '69 • We Will Rock You • You Ain't Seen Nothin' Yet • and lots more!
00240108 C Instruments....................$35.00

Classical Fake Book

This unprecedented, amazingly comprehensive reference includes over 850 classical themes and melodies for all classical music lovers. Includes everything from Renaissance music to Vivaldi and Mozart to Mendelssohn. Lyrics in the original language are included when appropriate.
00240044....................$39.99

The Disney Fake Book

Even more Disney favorites, including: The Bare Necessities • Can You Feel the Love Tonight • Circle of Life • How Do You Know? • Let It Go • Part of Your World • Reflection • Some Day My Prince Will Come • When I See an Elephant Fly • You'll Be in My Heart • and many more.
00175311 C Instruments...........$34.99

Disney characters & artwork TM & © 2021 Disney

The Folksong Fake Book

Over 1,000 folksongs: Bury Me Not on the Lone Prairie • Clementine • The Erie Canal • Go, Tell It on the Mountain • Home on the Range • Kumbaya • Michael Row the Boat Ashore • Shenandoah • Simple Gifts • Swing Low, Sweet Chariot • When Johnny Comes Marching Home • Yankee Doodle • and many more.
00240151....................$34.99

The Hal Leonard Real Jazz Standards Fake Book

Over 250 standards in easy-to-read authentic hand-written jazz engravings: Ain't Misbehavin' • Blue Skies • Crazy He Calls Me • Desafinado (Off Key) • Fever • How High the Moon • It Don't Mean a Thing (If It Ain't Got That Swing) • Lazy River • Mood Indigo • Old Devil Moon • Route 66 • Satin Doll • Witchcraft • and more.
00240161 C Instruments........................$45.00

The Hymn Fake Book

Nearly 1,000 multi-denominational hymns perfect for church musicians or hobbyists: Amazing Grace • Christ the Lord Is Risen Today • For the Beauty of the Earth • It Is Well with My Soul • A Mighty Fortress Is Our God • O for a Thousand Tongues to Sing • Praise to the Lord, the Almighty • Take My Life and Let It Be • What a Friend We Have in Jesus • and hundreds more!
00240145 C Instruments........................$29.99

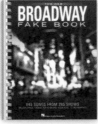

The New Broadway Fake Book

This amazing collection includes 645 songs from 285 shows: All I Ask of You • Any Dream Will Do • Close Every Door • Consider Yourself • Dancing Queen • Mack the Knife • Mamma Mia • Memory • The Phantom of the Opera • Popular • Strike up the Band • and more!
00138905 C Instruments............$45.00

The Praise & Worship Fake Book

Over 400 songs including: Amazing Grace (My Chains Are Gone) • Cornerstone • Everlasting God • Great Are You Lord • In Christ Alone • Mighty to Save • Open the Eyes of My Heart • Shine, Jesus, Shine • This Is Amazing Grace • and more.
00160838 C Instruments...........$39.99
00240324 B♭ Instruments.........$34.99

Three Chord Songs Fake Book

200 classic and contemporary 3-chord tunes in melody/lyric/chord format: Ain't No Sunshine • Bang a Gong (Get It On) • Cold, Cold Heart • Don't Worry, Be Happy • Give Me One Reason • I Got You (I Feel Good) • Kiss • Me and Bobby McGee • Rock This Town • Werewolves of London • You Don't Mess Around with Jim • and more.
00240387....................$34.99

The Ultimate Christmas Fake Book

The 6th edition of this bestseller features over 270 traditional and contemporary Christmas hits: Have Yourself a Merry Little Christmas • I'll Be Home for Christmas O Come, All Ye Faithful (Adeste Fideles) • Santa Baby • Winter Wonderland • and more.
00147215 C Instruments...........$30.00

The Ultimate Country Fake Book

This book includes over 700 of your favorite country hits: Always on My Mind • Boot Scootin' Boogie • Crazy • Down at the Twist and Shout • Forever and Ever, Amen • Friends in Low Places • The Gambler • Jambalaya • King of the Road • Sixteen Tons • There's a Tear in My Beer • Your Cheatin' Heart • and hundreds more.
00240049 C Instruments....................$49.99

The Ultimate Fake Book

Includes over 1,200 hits: Blue Skies • Body and Soul • Endless Love • Isn't It Romantic? • Memory • Mona Lisa • Moon River • Operator • Piano Man • Roxanne • Satin Doll • Shout • Small World • Smile • Speak Softly, Love • Strawberry Fields Forever • Tears in Heaven • Unforgettable • hundreds more!
00240024 C Instruments...........$55.00
00240026 B♭ Instruments....................$49.95

The Ultimate Jazz Fake Book

This must-own collection includes 635 songs spanning all jazz styles from more than 9 decades. Songs include: Maple Leaf Rag • Basin Street Blues • A Night in Tunisia • Lullaby of Birdland • The Girl from Ipanema • Bag's Groove • I Can't Get Started • All the Things You Are • and many more!
00240079 C Instruments...............$45.00
00240080 B♭ Instruments....................$45.00
00240081 E♭ Instruments....................$45.00

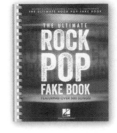

The Ultimate Rock Pop Fake Book

This amazing collection features nearly 550 rock and pop hits: American Pie • Bohemian Rhapsody • Born to Be Wild • Clocks • Dancing with Myself • Eye of the Tiger • Proud Mary • Rocket Man • Should I Stay or Should I Go • Total Eclipse of the Heart • Unchained Melody • When Doves Cry • Y.M.C.A. • You Raise Me Up • and more.
00240310 C Instruments....................$39.99

Complete songlists available online at
www.halleonard.com

HAL•LEONARD®

0421
Prices, contents & availabilty subject to change without notice
229